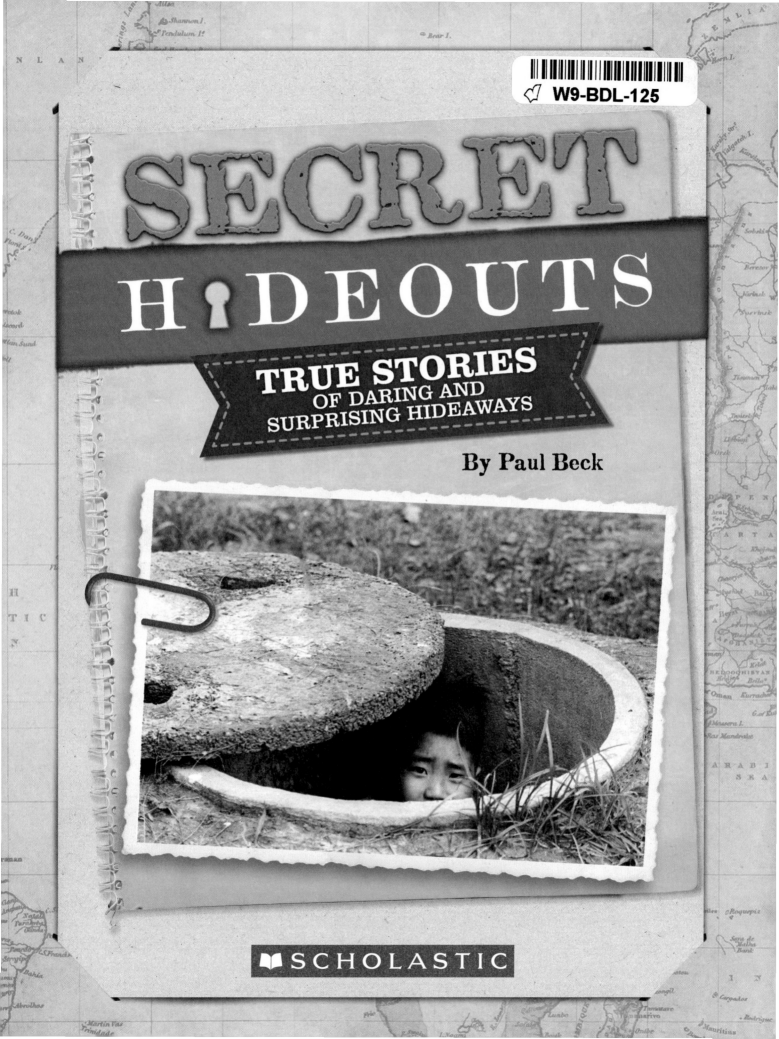

SECRET HIDEOUTS

TRUE STORIES
OF DARING AND SURPRISING HIDEAWAYS

By Paul Beck

SCHOLASTIC

an imprint of
SCHOLASTIC
www.scholastic.com

Published by Tangerine Press, an imprint of Scholastic Inc.,
557 Broadway, New York, NY 10012
Scholastic Canada Ltd., Markham, Ontario
Scholastic UK, Coventry, Warwickshire

Secret Hideouts is produced by becker&mayer! LLC
11120 NE 33rd Place, Suite 101
Bellevue, WA 98004
www.beckermayer.com

If you have questions or comments about this product, please visit
www.beckermayer.com/customerservice and click on Customer Service Request Form.

Author: Paul Beck
Editor: Delia Greve
Designers: Sarah Baynes and Megan Sugiyama
Production coordinator: Tom Miller
Photo researchers: Emily Zach & Jessica Eskelson

Printed, manufactured, and assembled in Jefferson City, MO, USA

10 9 8 7 6 5 4 3 2 1

ISBN: 978-0-545-73527-8

14035

Table of Contents

HIDING OUT

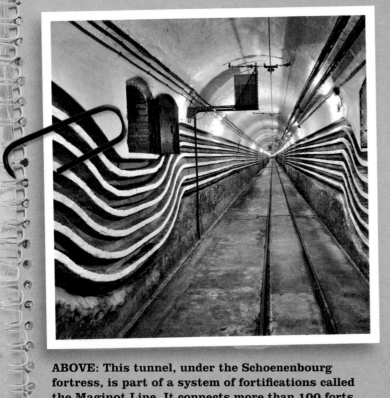

ABOVE: This tunnel, under the Schoenenbourg fortress, is part of a system of fortifications called the Maginot Line. It connects more than 100 forts along the eastern border of France.

WHAT MAKES A GOOD HIDING PLACE?

For starters, it's a place that can't be found easily. Sometimes it's enough for a hideaway to be remote and hard to reach, like on an island or deep within a desert canyon. Another smart hiding strategy is to go underground in caves or tunnels. The trickiest hideouts are hidden spaces behind walls, under floors, and in the attics of ordinary-looking buildings.

LEFT: Some hiding places are nearly impossible to get to, like the twisty desert canyons of Robbers Roost in Utah. Or they might be a whole subterranean city, like this carved-out tunnel in the Cheyenne Mountain military complex in Colorado Springs, Colorado.

ABOVE: Anne Frank and her family hid from the Nazis during World War II in a secret apartment above a warehouse in Amsterdam. LEFT: The pirate Blackbeard was known to hide out on the island of New Providence in the Bahamas.

WHY HIDE?

People hide for all kinds of reasons. Sometimes the "good guys" hide from "bad guys." Sometimes the "bad guys," like pirates or crooks, hide from the police or other authorities. Sometimes soldiers hide from the enemy. And sometimes people hide just to keep their secrets . . . secret.

THE GREAT PYRAMID

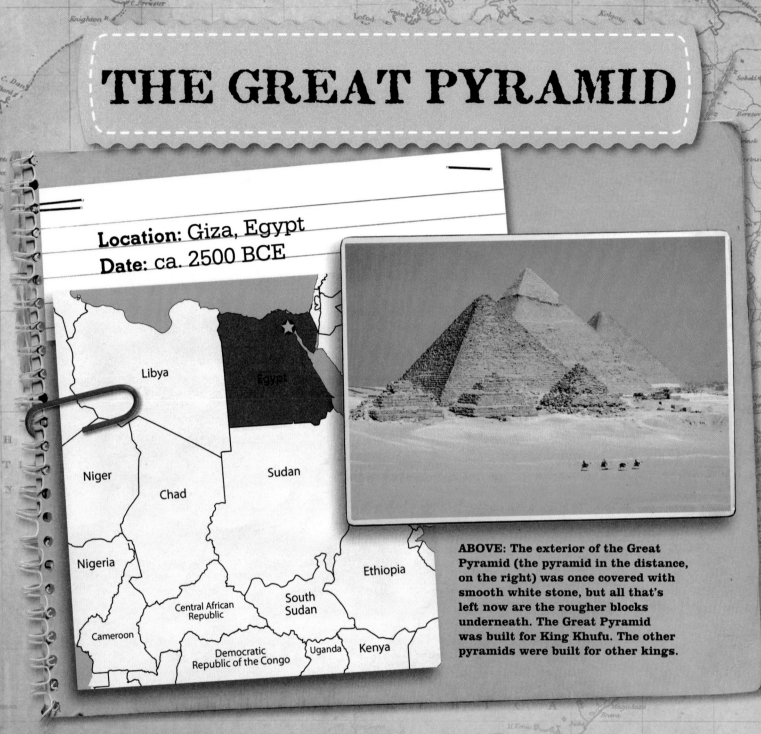

Location: Giza, Egypt

Date: ca. 2500 BCE

Libya
Egypt
Niger
Chad
Sudan
Nigeria
Ethiopia
Central African Republic
South Sudan
Cameroon
Democratic Republic of the Congo
Uganda
Kenya

ABOVE: The exterior of the Great Pyramid (the pyramid in the distance, on the right) was once covered with smooth white stone, but all that's left now are the rougher blocks underneath. The Great Pyramid was built for King Khufu. The other pyramids were built for other kings.

KING KHUFU

Deep inside the Great Pyramid are chambers built to hide the mummy and treasures of the Egyptian king, or pharaoh, named Khufu. Pharaohs had pyramids built to house their mummy and their possessions—food, clothes, jewelry, furniture, and other valuables—that they believed they would need in the afterlife. Once the mummy and treasures were placed in the tomb, the pyramid was sealed to protect its contents from robbers. Despite all that sealing and hiding, tomb robbers eventually tunneled their way into the pyramid, stealing the mummy of Khufu and all his treasures.

The Great Pyramid towers **480 ft. (146 m)** above the desert!

BELOW: Once the mummy and his treasures were placed in the Great Pyramid, three huge granite slabs were slid over the opening to seal the chamber. Then a block of stone was placed at the opening of the outside passage. This stone made the entrance invisible.

ABOVE: Passageways in the Great Pyramid led up through a tall gallery into the room now known as the King's Chamber. BELOW: Like most pharaohs, King Tut was laid to rest in a sarcophagus, or stone coffin.

KING TUT

The famous boy king, Tutankhamun, lived more than 1,200 years after Khufu. By that time, the Egyptians were no longer building pyramids. Instead, the pharaohs of King Tut's time were buried in tombs carved into cliffs in the Valley of the Kings, near the ancient city of Thebes. Tutankhamun's mummy and treasures stayed hidden until his tomb was excavated in the 1920s.

TROJAN HORSE

Location: Troy/Modern Turkey
Date: ca 1200 BCE

ABOVE: The Trojans argued about what to do with the wooden horse the Greeks left behind—should they chop it up with axes, throw it off a cliff into the sea, or offer it to the gods? The Trojans decided to keep the colossal horse, and brought it into their city. **BOTTOM:** The Trojan War began when a prince, named Paris, kidnapped Helen, the queen of Sparta, pictured here, and brought her to Troy.

TROJAN WAR

One of the most famous hideout stories comes from the ancient Greek legends about the Trojan War. According to the poem *The Odyssey* by Homer, a prince named Paris kidnapped Helen, queen of Sparta, and took her to the city of Troy. To get her back, the Greeks attacked Troy, but they couldn't fight their way inside the walled city. After 10 years of war, the Greeks sailed away. It looked as if they had given up. The only thing they left behind was a mysterious, giant wooden horse.

SNEAK ATTACK

The Trojans never guessed the horse's secret. A band of Greek soldiers had hidden themselves in the hollow body. When night fell and the horse was safely inside the city walls, the soldiers crept out of their hiding place led by the crafty warrior Odysseus. Meanwhile, the rest of the Greek soldiers came sneaking back in their boats. The warriors opened the city gates, and the army poured in. The Greeks sacked the city and won the Trojan War.

Today a *Trojan horse* can also refer to an e-mail, picture, or computer file that holds a hidden computer virus.

ABOVE: The Greek soldiers hidden in the Trojan horse waited until dark and then emerged to attack the city of Troy. RIGHT: Archaeologists have discovered the remains of what they think was the city of Troy from the stories in what is now Turkey. No traces of a wooden horse have been found.

JEWISH REBEL HIDEAWAYS

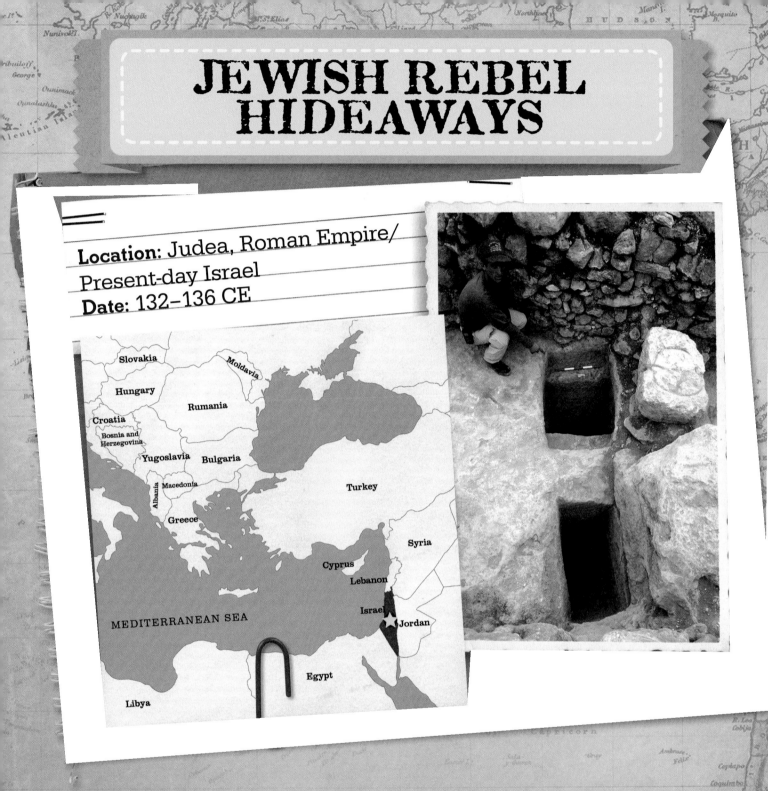

Location: Judea, Roman Empire/
Present-day Israel
Date: 132–136 CE

MAZELIKE TUNNELS

When Jewish inhabitants in the province of Judea rebelled against the Roman Empire, the fighters had no hope of defeating the Roman army on the battlefield. Instead, they fought in raids and small skirmishes, striking out from mountain caves and human-built underground hideouts. By carving tunnels in the soft limestone, the rebels connected underground chambers, turning the spaces into mazelike hideouts. The tunnel entrances were camouflaged. And once safely inside, the rebels would block the entrances with stone slabs or wooden beams. If any Roman soldier happened to get inside, the chances of him finding his way around were slim.

LEFT: The complex tunnels were small like burrows, so people could move through them only by crawling or sliding.

UNDERGROUND LIVING

The rebels could stay holed up in the hiding complexes for a long time. They had plenty of food and water, and ventilation shafts brought in air. There were storage rooms for grain and other food, cisterns for collecting water, quarries, baths, and rooms called columbaria (singular: columbarium), where the ashes of the dead were placed. The revolt was successful at first. The rebels drove out the Romans and set up a Jewish state, but the Roman Emperor Hadrian eventually sent in a huge army and crushed the rebellion.

ABOVE: The rooms and connecting tunnels had many twists, turns, and level changes. **BELOW:** Archaeologists have also found papyrus documents and coins from the period.

Archaeologists have found more than **320 Roman-era hideaways!**

THE UNDERGROUND KREMLIN

Location: Moscow, Russia

Date: 1485–1495

LE KREMLIN EST UNE VILLE ET UNE CITADELLE

LEFT: The Moscow Kremlin is a group of palaces, churches, and other buildings surrounded by a high fortress wall.

Russia

Kazakhstan
Mongolia
Uzbekistan
Kyrgyzstan
Turkey
Turkmenistan
Syria
China
Iraq
Afghanistan
Iran
Japan
Saudi Arabia
Pakistan
Nepal
India
Burma (Myanmar)

WALLED IN SECRECY

The Moscow Kremlin is made up of several buildings surrounded by a high wall. It is like a small city within the larger city of Moscow that houses the government of Russia. When the Kremlin was being built, medieval builders constructed secret rooms and underground passageways. Some tunnels, called *tainiks*, led down to the Moscow River or out into the city. The tunnels could be used to bring water into the Kremlin, to escape during a siege, or to travel to and from the fortress in secret. Big, padlocked doors separated some of the passages into shorter sections where the royal family and Russian nobles stored gold, silver, jewels, and other treasures in vaults under the fortress. As new buildings were added and old ones were torn down, many of the underground passages were blocked by construction or sealed up and forgotten. Over the years, archaeologists have tried to explore the underground Kremlin, but most of the hiding places remain shrouded in secrecy.

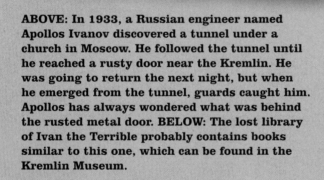

ABOVE: In 1933, a Russian engineer named Apollos Ivanov discovered a tunnel under a church in Moscow. He followed the tunnel until he reached a rusty door near the Kremlin. He was going to return the next night, but when he emerged from the tunnel, guards caught him. Apollos has always wondered what was behind the rusted metal door. BELOW: The lost library of Ivan the Terrible probably contains books similar to this one, which can be found in the Kremlin Museum.

Along the passageway Apollos discovered two small rooms with skeletons inside.

THE LOST LIBRARY

Ivan IV, better known as Ivan the Terrible, was the first Russian ruler to call himself *tsar*, or emperor. Ivan inherited hundreds of ancient books and manuscripts. He collected hundreds more himself. Legend has it that to protect his priceless library from thieves, invaders, and fire, the tsar sealed the manuscripts in secret vaults beneath the Kremlin. Ivan the Terrible died in 1584. No one has ever found his library.

THE PASSETTO DI BORGO

Location: Vatican City/Rome, Italy

Date: Middle Ages

LEFT: The most famous escape through the Passetto was during an attack by renegade soldiers. BELOW: The Passetto di Borgo is an elevated walkway that runs through Rome.

POPE CLEMENT VII'S ESCAPE

In 1527, a huge army of renegade soldiers attacked Rome. They broke through its defensive walls and began to loot the city. Pope Clement VII was in St. Peter's Basilica when the invaders descended. The pope rushed toward a secret passageway called the Passetto di Borgo to escape the church. With his robe draped over one arm, Clement hurried along the narrow corridor. After rushing along the passageway, Pope Clement reached the stronghold named Castel Sant'Angelo. He was safe!

THE PASSAGE

The Passetto di Borgo runs inside a thick stone wall. The wall stretches from Vatican City to the Castel Sant'Angelo on the banks of the Tiber River. The wall was built in the Middle Ages. It was part of fortifications that surrounded the whole Vatican. At first the Passetto was an open walkway on top of the wall. Later it was covered over by another walkway, and the Passetto became an enclosed passageway inside the wall.

The passage is 2,625 ft (800 m) long.

ABOVE: The Passetto was built for emergencies, in case the pope needed a quick escape route from his apartments to the fortified castle. Clement VII was the last pope to use it that way. LEFT: The Passetto begins in Vatican City and ends here at Castel Sant'Angelo, which means "Castle of the Holy Angel."

PRIEST HOLES

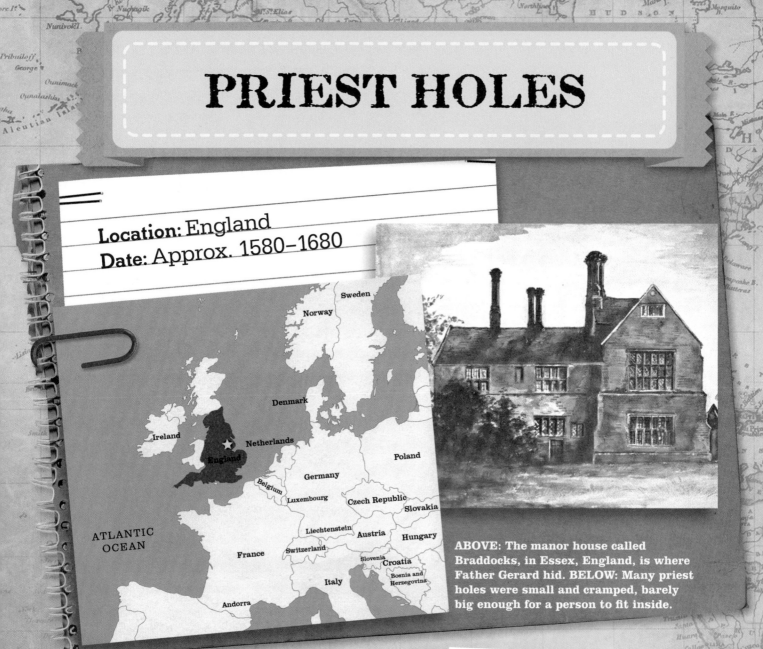

Location: England
Date: Approx. 1580–1680

ABOVE: The manor house called Braddocks, in Essex, England, is where Father Gerard hid. BELOW: Many priest holes were small and cramped, barely big enough for a person to fit inside.

FATHER JOHN GERARD

Squeezed into a tiny hideout beneath a fake floor in a fireplace, Father John Gerard held his breath. The priest hunters were literally right on top of him. Father Gerard was a Catholic priest. At that time, the Catholic religion was illegal in England. The penalty was death. But many people practiced the Catholic religion in secret. Some manor houses had hidden chapels or secret hideouts, called priest holes, where a priest could hide inside the wall, floor, attic, cellar, or other secret space while the queen's priest hunters searched the house. Father Gerard hid under the fireplace for four days without food, water, or sleep while the priest hunters searched the house. He emerged when the priest hunters finally left, weak but still alive and free.

LEFT: The priest's hiding hole in a staircase at Sawston Hall designed and made by Nicholas Owen. BELOW: Priests often hid for days in cramped quarters to avoid priest hunters.

THE MASTER HIDER

Nicholas Owen was a Catholic brother and a master builder of priest holes. He created hideouts in places so small no one would ever guess a person could fit inside them. His carpentry, stonework, and painting tricks were so good, priest hunters couldn't find the entrances, even when they were looking right at them. To disguise his secret work, he would do carpentry on some part of the house during the day. Then he would do his hideout work at night. Nicholas Owen would never tell anyone about the hideouts he built, not even another Catholic.

TORTUGA

Location: Tortuga (part of present-day Haiti)
Date: 1640–1654

Florida

Bahamas

Cuba

Haiti

Dominican Republic

Tortuga means **"turtle"** in Spanish.

ABOVE: Tortuga was both a hideout and the pirate capital of the Caribbean. From the water the island looks like the back of a giant sea turtle. BELOW: The buccaneer pirates of Tortuga called themselves the Brethren of the Coast.

BECOMING A PIRATE

The story of the pirate island of Tortuga began with French and English hunters who lived on the north shore of Hispaniola. The hunters traded meat and hides from the pigs and wild cattle that lived on the island with Spanish colonists who also lived on the island. The hunters smoked the meat on wooden grates called *boucans.* Thus the hunters came to be known in French as *boucaniers*—or, in English, *buccaneers.* When the hunting was lean, some buccaneers would raid passing ships, stealing their cargo. When the Spanish colonists on Hispaniola tried to drive them off the island by wiping out the wild cattle, the buccaneers took to raiding ships full-time and moved to Tortuga.

The buccaneers ruled their island hideout for 14 years.

ABOVE: The island's rocky coast and a fort with cannons provided protection for the pirates against outside attacks. BELOW: Before starting on a voyage, all members of a pirate crew signed an agreement that specified how the loot would be divided.

THE PIRATE CAPITAL

Pirates used Tortuga as their home base, sailing out from its harbor to attack ships. The best prizes were Spanish ships loaded with gold, silver, and other treasures on their way home to Europe. The pirates would then return to Tortuga to spend their money and refit their ships for the next raid. As stories spread, would-be pirates flocked to Tortuga until an all-out effort by Spanish warships drove them away. But the pirates soon found other places to hide out and continued their plundering ways.

Articles of Agreement

1. Every man shall have equal voting rights.
2. Every man shall have a proper share of the loot. If any man cheats the company or fellow man even one dollar, he shall be marooned.
3. None shall game for money either with dice or cards.
4. All lights or candles should be out at eight o'clock.
5. Every man shall keep his weapon cleaned and ready for action.
6. No boy or woman is allowed onboard.
7. Any man that deserts the ship or his quarters in time of battle shall be punished by death or marooning.
8. No man shall strike another on board the ship.
9. No man shall talk of breaking up their way of living till each has a share of 1,000. Every man who becomes a cripple or loses a limb shall have 800 pieces of eight from the common stock.
10. The captain and the quartermaster shall each receive two shares of a prize, the master gunner and boatswain, one and one half shares, all others, one and one quarter, and private gentlemen one share each.

MOSELEY OLD HALL

Location: Staffordshire, England

Date: 1651

ABOVE: The upstairs bedroom at Moseley Old Hall, an English manor house, has a priest hole where Charles II hid from British soldiers. BELOW: The room where King Charles stayed at Moseley Old Hall.

HIDING A KING

On a September day in 1651, a young man named Charles rested in a guest room at Moseley Old Hall. Suddenly, he heard his host shout, "Soldiers! Soldiers are coming!" Charles ran to a hidden door in the wall and lowered himself into a dark hiding place. The hiding place was a priest hole, but now it held a future king. When the British rebels called Roundheads took over the English government, they abolished the English monarchy. The 21-year-old Charles knew if he were caught, he would be beheaded like his father, King Charles I. Those who were loyal to the king were trying to get him safely out of England. Charles waited a long time in the dark for his host to let him know it was safe to emerge from his hiding place.

Charles was **21 years old** when he fled to France.

ABOVE: The Moseley Old Hall priest hole was located under a secret panel in the floor of a closet behind a secret door. BELOW: After Charles II returned to England, he ruled for 25 years.

KING CHARLES II

Once Charles emerged from the priest hole, he fled across the countryside, traveling in disguise. It took him more than a month to reach the English Channel, where he sailed to safety in France. Charles lived in exile in France for nearly nine years. Two years after Oliver Cromwell, the leader of the Roundheads, died, the British parliament voted to restore the monarchy. They invited Charles to come back. He returned to England to become King Charles II.

QUILOMBO DOS PALMARES

Location: Quilombo dos Palmares, Brazil

Date: 1605–1694

LEFT: Palmares was the largest community of escaped slaves in Brazil. It was about 40 mi. (64.3 km) inland from the coast in the northeast part of the country.

Maroon comes from the Spanish word *cimarrón*, meaning "runaway."

ESCAPING TO FREEDOM

Brazil was the center of the slave trade between Africa and the Americas. Twelve times as many slaves were brought there as to the English-speaking parts of North America. Most of the slaves in Brazil were forced to work in gold mines or on sugar plantations. More than a third of them died within five years. But many slaves managed to escape.

They vanished into the interior of the country, where thick forest and a maze of rivers protected them. As more and more slaves escaped to freedom into the forests, they began to live together in settlements called Maroon communities. The Brazilian Portuguese word for a Maroon community is *quilombo* (kee-LOM-boo).

LEFT: The largest *quilombo* compound had 220 buildings, with a wall of wooden stakes around the outside. BELOW: Zumbi, last leader of Palmares, is a Brazilian national hero. The airport in Maceió, near the old Palmares *quilombo*, is named Zumbi dos Palmares in his honor.

THE MAROON SETTLEMENT

The biggest and longest-lasting *quilombo* in Brazil was called Palmares. As more and more slaves escaped, the *quilombo* grew into a hideout colony the size of Massachusetts. The colony had several separate compounds called *mocambos*, meaning "hideout" in the Kimbundu language of Africa. The inhabitants forged metal farming tools and grew crops. At its height, Palmares was home to as many as 30,000 people, ruled by a king. The last leader of Palmares was named Zumbi. Even after the colony was conquered in 1694, Zumbi continued to fight against slavery.

The *quilombo* of Palmares lasted almost **100 years.**

NEW PROVIDENCE

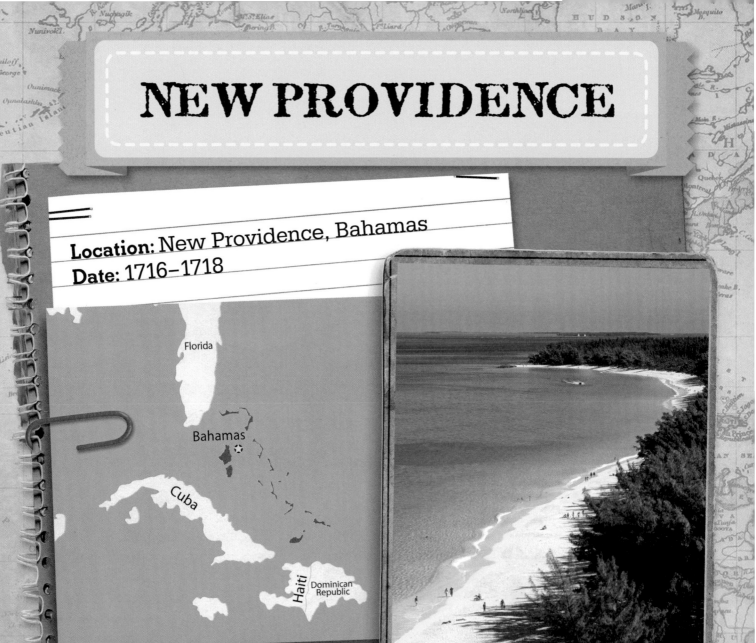

Location: New Providence, Bahamas
Date: 1716–1718

Florida

Bahamas

Cuba

Haiti

Dominican Republic

RIGHT: The former pirate town by the harbor on New Providence island is now known as Nassau.

THE PIRATE HAVEN

New Providence was an excellent pirate hideout. Even though the Bahamas belonged to Britain in the early 1700s, there was no government to speak of on the islands. By 1716, pirates had taken over the island. They set up their own cannons on the walls of the fort, commanding the harbor and the town. By 1717, there were between 800 and 2,000 pirates based in New Providence, including such famous captains as Stede Bonnet, Calico Jack Rackham, and Edward Teach (better known as Blackbeard). However, New Providence's reign as a pirate hideout was a short one.

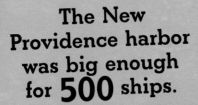

LEFT: Captain Woodes Rogers sailed into New Providence harbor with a small flotilla of navy ships to clean out the nest of pirates.

The New Providence harbor was big enough for **500** ships.

KING GEORGE'S PARDON

On July 26, 1718, a British man-of-war and three smaller navy ships sailed into the harbor of New Providence. Captain Woodes Rogers carried a proclamation by King George I of England. The proclamation said any pirate who pledged to give up his plundering ways would receive a full pardon. Most of the outlaws took the pardon and swore off piracy. Of course, many of them went back to their old ways as soon as they sailed out of the harbor. But over the next four years, the British navy stamped out most of the outlaws, and the Golden Age of Piracy was over.

ABOVE: New Providence-based pirate Captain Charles Vane wanted nothing to do with the King's pardon. When Rogers arrived, he lit one of his ships on fire and set it drifting toward the navy ships, while he used the distraction to sail out of the harbor.

SNOW'S ISLAND

Location: Snow's Island, South Carolina
Date: 1780–1781

ABOVE: The Pee Dee river near where experts believe Snow's Island to be located.

ISLAND HIDEOUT

During the American Revolution, General Francis Marion was infamous for his sneak attacks. Marion and his men would appear as if from nowhere, ambush the British, and disappear back into the swampy forest. Marion operated from his headquarters on Snow's Island in the Pee Dee River. He and his fighters would make scouting trips and mount attacks from the island. To make his headquarters harder to find, Marion destroyed bridges and blocked roads in the region around the island. Marion's attacks caused so much trouble for the British, they grew determined to destroy his hideout. One early spring day, a British force attacked Snow's Island and wrecked the camp. Marion didn't use the hideout again.

ABOVE: Marion and his men crossed to and from the hideout. Marion's horse, Ball, was an especially good swimmer.

THE SWAMP FOX

Francis Marion got his nickname, the Swamp Fox, from a British colonel who was pursuing him and a group of his fighters. After a 26-mi. (42-km) chase, Marion and his men disappeared into the swamp.

One of the Swamp Fox's greatest attacks was at Nelson's Ferry. A group of British soldiers was camped by an inn near Nelson's Ferry, escorting a group of captured American soldiers. When everyone was asleep, American fighters charged from the trees. There was a short battle, but the redcoats quickly surrendered.

ABOVE: The surprise attack at Nelson's Ferry was just one of many led by the Swamp Fox.

DOVER CASTLE TUNNELS

Location: Dover, England

Date: 1803–1990s

ABOVE: The Napoleonic-era tunnel system (in blue) was expanded with extra tunnels during World War II (in red). **BELOW:** Dover Castle today.

The original tunnels are
70 ft. (21 m)
below the cliff top!

UNDERGROUND TUNNELS

Dover Castle sits atop white cliffs, and looks out over the Straits of Dover, the narrowest part of the English Channel between England and France. The fortress was built around 1160 by King Henry II. In the early 1800s, the French leader Napoleon was conquering large swaths of Europe. England's military feared a French attack, so they decided to modernize the medieval castle with state-of-the-art artillery. But there wasn't room in the castle for the soldiers who would man the guns. The army dug seven parallel tunnels under the castle to hold as many as 2,000 soldiers. The tunnels were finished in 1803, but as it turned out, Napoleon never attacked.

ADDING TO THE MAZE

At the beginning of World War II, the tunnels were put to use as the headquarters for the Dover Naval Command. Vice Admiral Bertram Ramsay used the tunnels as command center for Operation Dynamo—a plan to evacuate British soldiers stranded on the French beaches near the city of Dunkirk. He expected to rescue about 45,000 soldiers. Instead, Operation Dynamo brought back 338,000 soldiers!

RIGHT: During the Cold War of the 1950s, even more tunnels were added. The underground hideout became a shelter to house part of the British government in the event of a nuclear war. BELOW: The repeater room in the subterranean tunnels used to amplify telephone messages during World War II. Now the tunnels are a museum.

MOUNT ZION AME CHURCH

Location: Woolwich Township, New Jersey

Date: 1834–1864

LEFT: Located in southwestern New Jersey, the Mount Zion Church was very close to the slave state of Delaware, just across the Delaware River.

There was a knock on the church door. A man opened the door a crack to check who was there. Four figures stood huddled together. As soon as the door closed behind them, the man lifted a hidden trap door in the floor of the church. He helped the four newcomers climb through the opening. Then, he handed down a jug of water and a sack of food, and closed the trap door over them. If the slave catchers came, they wouldn't be found . . .

UNDERGROUND RAILROAD

It was 1851. The Mount Zion AME (African Methodist Episcopal) Church was a station on the Underground Railroad. The Underground Railroad wasn't really underground, and it wasn't a railroad. It was a system of hideouts, escape routes, and people who helped runaway slaves flee from the South to freedom in Canada. It was a crime for anyone to help or give shelter to a fugitive slave. Slave catchers from the South patrolled the escape routes, hoping to catch fugitives.

$150 REWARD

RANAWAY from the subscriber, on the night of the 2d instant, a negro man, who calls himself *Henry May*, about **22** years old, 5 feet 6 or 8 inches high, ordinary color, rather chunky built, bushy head, and has it divided mostly on one side, and keeps it very nicely combed; has been raised in the house, and is a first rate dining-room servant, and was in a tavern in Louisville for 18 months. I expect he is now in Louisville trying to make his escape to a free state, (in all probability to Cincinnati, Ohio.) Perhaps he may try to get employment on a steamboat. He is a good cook, and is handy in any capacity as a house servant. Had on when he left, a dark cassinett coatee, and dark striped cassinett pantaloons, new—he had other clothing. I will give $50 reward if taken in Louisvill; 100 dollars if taken one hundred miles from Louisville in this State, and 150 dollars if taken out of this State, and delivered to me, or secured in any jail so that I can get him again.   WILLIAM BURKE.

Bardstown, Ky., September 3d, 1838.

ABOVE LEFT: Slavery was illegal in the states of the North, but a federal law said any slave who escaped, even if he or she reached the free states, was still a slave and would be returned to the South. **ABOVE RIGHT:** Like many Underground Railroad stations, the church had a secret crawlspace where passengers on the Underground Railroad could hide. **LEFT:** Harriet Tubman helped more than 300 former slaves reach freedom.

HARRIET TUBMAN

Although many white abolitionists were part of the Underground Railroad, most of the people who helped slaves escape were free African Americans living in the North. One of the most famous of these Underground Railroad conductors was Harriet Tubman. Often disguising herself as an old woman or man to avoid capture, she helped more than 300 former slaves reach freedom.

THE SECRET SUBWAY

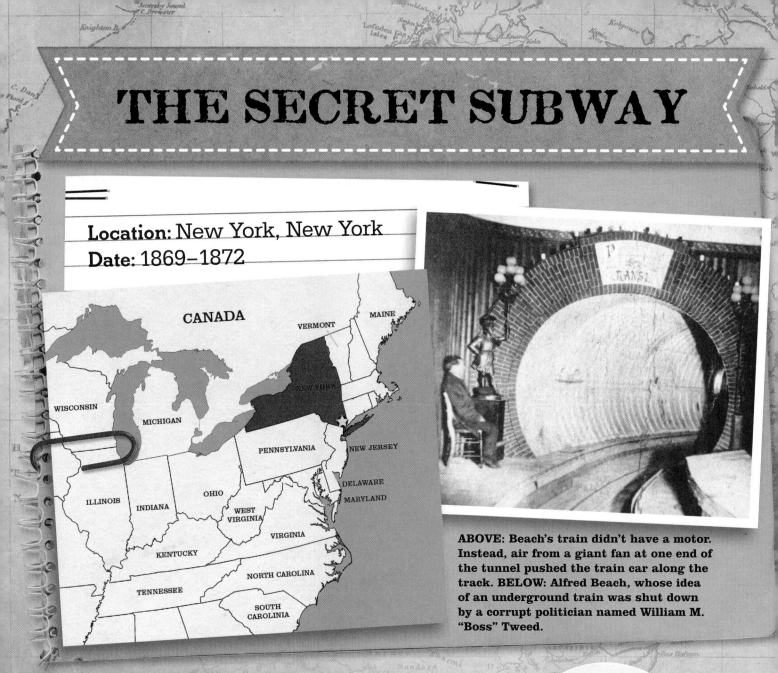

Location: New York, New York
Date: 1869–1872

ABOVE: Beach's train didn't have a motor. Instead, air from a giant fan at one end of the tunnel pushed the train car along the track. BELOW: Alfred Beach, whose idea of an underground train was shut down by a corrupt politician named William M. "Boss" Tweed.

A NEW WAY TO GET AROUND

Inventor Alfred Beach wanted to build a train in New York City—one that ran underground! But there was a problem. Beach couldn't get permission. So Beach rented the basement of a building across the street from City Hall and built a secret subway. Beach's workers dug a block-long tunnel in secret. When Beach revealed his train, it was a big hit. People stood in line to take the 25-cent ride, even though it was only a block long. Beach's mini-subway was shut down after three years, and the tunnel was sealed up. In 1912, workers were digging a new subway line in New York City and came across a bricked-up opening. Behind the bricks, they discovered Beach's air-powered subway car and the remains of the elegant station he had built.

A SECRET GLIMPSE

There's a secret subway station that visitors to New York City can see for themselves—the abandoned City Hall station, not far from where Alfred Beach dug his original secret tunnel. The station closed in 1945, but the Number 6 subway passes through it when the train loops around at the end of its line. The secret station is visible from the train to those who stay aboard after the last stop by the Brooklyn Bridge.

ABOVE: Beach's fully completed subway included a station decorated with chandeliers and a fountain. **RIGHT:** The abandoned City Hall station, not far from where Alfred Beach dug his original secret tunnel.

Beach wanted to expand his subway to **5 mi. (8 km),** but "Boss" Tweed shut it down.

SVBWAY ENTRANCE

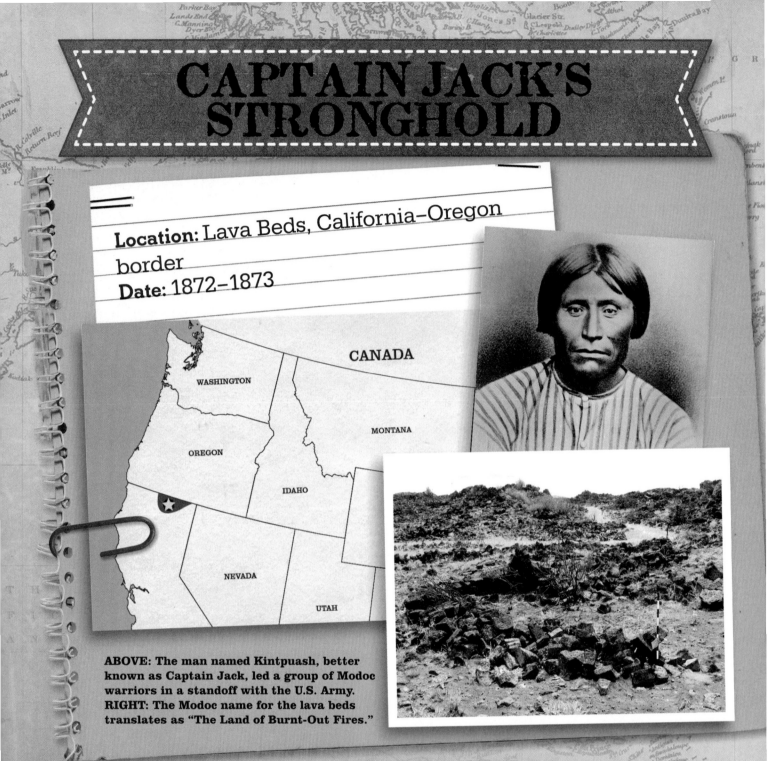

Location: Lava Beds, California–Oregon border
Date: 1872–1873

CANADA

WASHINGTON

MONTANA

OREGON

IDAHO

NEVADA

UTAH

**ABOVE: The man named Kintpuash, better known as Captain Jack, led a group of Modoc warriors in a standoff with the U.S. Army.
RIGHT: The Modoc name for the lava beds translates as "The Land of Burnt-Out Fires."**

CAPTAIN JACK'S STAND

Captain Jack's story isn't a happy one. The Modoc Native American Tribe had been persuaded to sign a treaty handing over their homeland in exchange for food, supplies, and reservation land. But the land they were given was shared with the Klamath Tribe. The Modoc and Klamath people didn't get along, so a group of Modocs decided to go back to their homeland on the California–Oregon border. The U.S. Army tried to force them back to the reservation, but the Modocs refused to go. Captain Jack led a group to an area of lava beds. Hidden in the maze of rocks, the band of just over 50 Modoc warriors held off more than 1,000 U.S. Army soldiers for nearly six months. Eventually, Captain Jack was captured, but the natural fortress became known as Captain Jack's Stronghold.

THE LAND OF BURNT-OUT FIRES

In Northern California, by the Oregon border, there is a rugged area of land called the lava beds. This rocky terrain was created by molten lava flows from the nearby Medicine Lake volcano. A maze of twisty paths winds through bluffs and crags of black rock. Caves riddle the landscape. They were formed tens of thousands of years ago when cooling lava hardened into tubes around the still-liquid rock flowing inside.

ABOVE: During the retreat, a small group of warriors killed some civilian settlers on the way to the stronghold. Captain Jack was angry with them, but he let them stay with the group. LEFT: A cave near Captain Jack's Stronghold.

ROBBERS ROOST

Location: Robbers Roost, Utah
Date: 1870s–early 1900s

$4,000 Reward
WILL BE PAID FOR THE CAPTURE OF ROBERT LEROY PARKER
DEAD OR ALIVE

Age, 36 years (1901)
Weight, 165 lbs.
Complexion, Light.
Eyes, Blue.
Nationality, American.
Marks, two cut scars back
head, small scar under
left eye, small brown
mole calf of leg.

Height, 5 ft. 9 in.
Build, Medium.
Color of hair, Flaxen.
Mustache, sandy if any.
Occupation,
Cowboy, Rustler.
Criminal occupation,
bank robber & Highwayman,
cattle and horse thief.

ROBERT LEROY PARKER
ALIAS
"BUTCH" CASSIDY

Is known as a criminal principally in Wyoming, Utah, Idaho, Colorado & Nevada
and has served time in Wyoming State Penitentiary at Laramie for grand larceny,
but was pardoned Jan. 19, 1896. Wanted for robbery First National Bank.
WINNEMUCCA, NEVADA, September 19, 1900.

LEFT: Robert Leroy Parker, a.k.a. Butch Cassidy, was the leader of the outlaw gang the Wild Bunch.

DOWN IN THE CANYON

In 1874, a horse thief named Cap Brown was looking for a place to keep his stolen animals. It had to be somewhere the law couldn't find him. He found an ideal hideout: a plateau in the high desert of southeastern Utah with deep, twisting canyons. Over the years, other thieves started using the area to hide their stolen goods. Thus, the hideout became known as Robbers Roost. The most famous outlaw to use the area was Butch Cassidy's gang, the Wild Bunch. The bandits built a corral there for their horses and left caches of supplies in the red canyons. Robbers Roost got a reputation as a dangerous place because of both the treacherous terrain and the ruthless outlaws.

Legend says "Flat Nose" George Curry hid **$65,000** in the canyons, but met his untimely end before he could get back to it.

THE WILD BUNCH

Cattle rustlers Robert Leroy Parker and Mike Cassidy used Robbers Roost to stash livestock. Parker liked the work and became a full-time outlaw in 1884. He took a new name in honor of his old partner. He called himself Butch Cassidy.

During their career of crime, Butch Cassidy and the Wild Bunch committed the longest string of bank, train, and payroll robberies in the history of the West. Other members of the gang included Harry Longabaugh, otherwise known as the Sundance Kid, Elzy Lay, and Harvey Logan, alias Kid Curry.

ABOVE: The Wild Bunch. Seated left to right: Harry Longabaugh, Ben Kilpatrick, Butch Cassidy. Standing left to right: William Carver, Harvey Logan. LEFT: Robbers Roost is still one of the most remote and rugged places in the West. It's near the towns of Green River and Moab, Utah. Part of the hideout area lies in Canyonlands National Park.

HOLE-IN-THE-WALL

Location: Hole-in-the-Wall, Wyoming
Date: 1860s–early 1900s

CANADA

MONTANA · NORTH DAKOTA · MINNESOTA · SOUTH DAKOTA · WYOMING · IOWA · NEBRASKA · COLORADO · KANSAS · ARIZONA · NEW MEXICO · OKLAHOMA

ABOVE: Butch Cassidy's and Harry Longabaugh's cabin from Hole-in-the-Wall, shown here, was relocated to just outside Cody, Wyoming. **BELOW:** Hole-in-the-Wall isn't all that hard to find for anyone who knows where to look. Its remote location is what made it a good hideout.

THE OUTLAW TOWN

In northern Wyoming, there is a long line of cliffs called the Red Wall. The only way through them is a V-shaped notch called the Hole-in-the-Wall. The trail from this pass descends into a grassy valley. The valley and hidden canyons around it are good areas for grazing cattle—especially if they're stolen cattle. Like Robbers Roost in Utah, Hole-in-the-Wall was an outlaw hideout. The first outlaw to use the area as a hideout may have been Sanford "Sang" Thompson. Later a group of outlaws called the Hole-in-the-Wall Gang used the hideout as its base. Butch Cassidy, the Sundance Kid, and the rest of the Wild Bunch came here, too. There were other, more law-abiding residents in Hole-in-the-Wall. But the outlaws left them alone. Eventually, when the gangs moved on, the honest homesteaders outnumbered the outlaws, and Hole-in-the-Wall's days as a hideout were over.

ABOVE: Members of Butch Cassidy's Wild Bunch included Laura Bullion, Harry Longabaugh (a.k.a. The Sundance Kid), Etta Place, and Jesse Linsley. RIGHT: The Wild Bunch pulled off their last big holdup when they robbed the Great Northern Flyer train in Montana in 1901. That same year, Butch Cassidy and the Sundance Kid went to South America. Even today, nobody knows what happened to them.

THE OUTLAW TRAIL

Hole-in-the-Wall is at the northern end of a route that was traveled often by the Wild Bunch and other outlaws. Known as the Outlaw Trail, it runs from Robbers Roost in Utah, in the south, through a hideout called Brown's Hole near the spot where the Colorado, Utah, and Wyoming borders meet, and then all the way north to Hole-in-the-Wall.

Great Northern Express Co.

ST. PAUL, MINN., JULY 4, 1901.

$5000 Reward

The Great Northern Railway "Overland" West-bound Train No. 3 was held up about three miles east of Wagner, Mont., Wednesday afternoon, July 3, 1901, and the Great Northern Express Company's through safe blown open with dynamite and the contents taken.

There were three men connected with the hold-up, described as follows:

One was, height 5 feet and 9 inches, weight about 175 pounds, blue eyes, had a projecting brow and about two weeks growth of sandy beard on chin, wore new tan shoes, black coat, corduroy trousers, and carried a silver plated, gold mounted Colt's revolver with a pearl handle.

Second man, height 6 feet, weight about 175 pounds, sandy complexion, blue eyes, not very large with slight cast in left eye; wore workingman's shoes, blue overalls over black suit of clothes, had a boot leg for cartridge pouch suspended from his neck.

Third man resembled a half breed very strongly, had large dark eyes, smoothly shaven face, and a very prominent nose; features clear cut, weight about 180 pounds, slightly stooped in shoulders, but very square across the shoulders, and wore a light slouch hat.

All three men used very marked Texas cowboy dialect, and two of them carried Winchester rifles, one of which was new. One had a carbine, same pattern as the Winchesters. They rode away on black, white, and buckskin horses respectively.

The Great Northern Express Company will give $5000 reward for the capture and identification of the three men, or a proportionate amount for one or two and $500 additional for each conviction.

D. S. ELLIOTT,
Auditor.

Approved:

D. MILLER,
President.

ELLINGTON SCHOOL

Location: Ramsgate, England
Date: 1917–1946

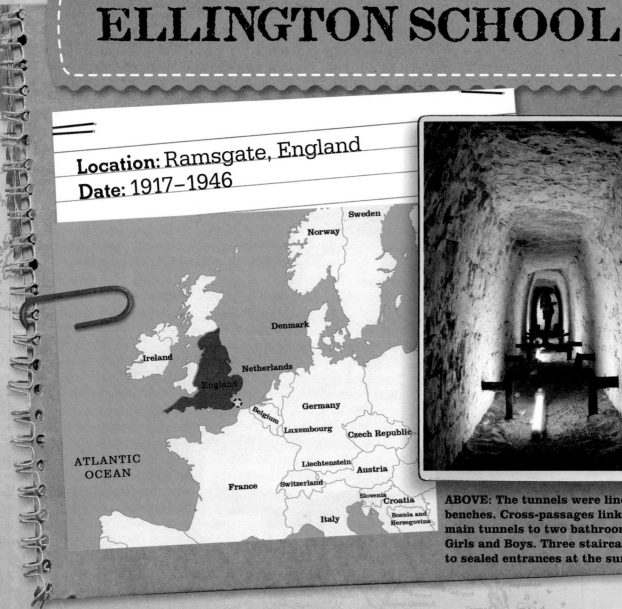

ABOVE: The tunnels were lined with benches. Cross-passages linked the two main tunnels to two bathrooms, marked Girls and Boys. Three staircases led up to sealed entrances at the surface.

AIR-RAID SHELTER

In April 2010, construction workers were digging on the site of a new housing development in Ramsgate, England. They broke through the roof of an underground space and found two parallel tunnels, 40 ft. (12 m) deep. The new development was being built on the former site of the Ellington School. The tunnels were part of an air-raid shelter, and were used as a hideout during World War I bombing raids. But the war ended soon after the shelter was finished, and it was closed up without ever being used. However, in 1944 during World War II, the air-raid shelter was reopened. Students from the school and others used it for protection from raids by German bombers. After the war, in 1946, the tunnels were sealed for safety.

England endured **247 days** of bombings during World War II.

LEFT: Bombings during World War II caused significant damage to buildings like this one hit during an air-raid in the Brixton area of London.
BELOW: Archaeologists also found graffiti on the walls of the air-raid shelter—some of the drawings were even signed by the students.

PUZZLING OUT THE PAST

There weren't any records from the school or the government showing when the air-raid shelter was used. Archaeologists figured it all out from graffiti! The students in the shelter had drawn and written on the walls. They left pictures, names, initials, and even homework assignments. Sometimes a graffitist also wrote his or her age, grade in school, or the date. Most of the dates were from 1944. There were also drawings making fun of students from a rival school named Saint George's. Someone had even drawn a couple of pictures of Popeye!

ARRAS MILITARY HIDEOUT

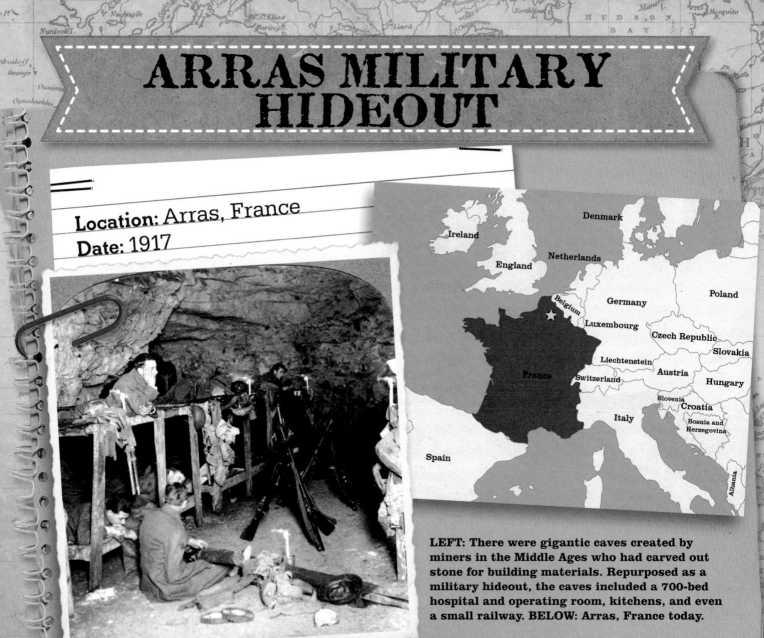

Location: Arras, France

Date: 1917

LEFT: There were gigantic caves created by miners in the Middle Ages who had carved out stone for building materials. Repurposed as a military hideout, the caves included a 700-bed hospital and operating room, kitchens, and even a small railway. BELOW: Arras, France today.

MILITARY HIDEOUT

Below a bakery in Arras, France, two doors led to ancient tunnels. Underneath the town there was a network of tunnels and caves. Some of them dated back to the Middle Ages and the others to the Roman Empire. During World War I, the British army was trying to break through German lines. The soldiers needed a place to gather and stay hidden. The officers decided to create a hideout for them by connecting the caves and quarries under Arras with new tunnels. In just a few months' time, army miners linked the medieval caves and ancient tunnels to create an underground city. When it was time, the soldiers entered the tunnels a few at a time, taking a whole week to filter in. Finally, on Easter 1917, the soldiers emerged from the tunnels, and the battle of Arras began.

ABOVE: The huge stone pillars in the quarry caves were marked with numbers to help soldiers find their way. RIGHT: Twenty-four thousand soldiers lived in the underground hideout for eight days, until they received the signal to attack.

THE DIGGING CREW

The tunnels were dug by 500 miners from the New Zealand Army Tunneling Company. They were joined by a group of "bantams," miners from Yorkshire, England, who were all shorter than the minimum height for the regular army— 5 ft. 2 in. (1.5 m). They named the different parts of the tunnels after their hometowns. The south part of the underground hideout got the names of cities in New Zealand, including Auckland and Wellington. The north part got the names of Scottish and English cities, including Edinburgh and London.

Army miners carved out **12 mi. (19.5 km)** of new tunnels.

Location: New York, New York
Date: 1920s–1933

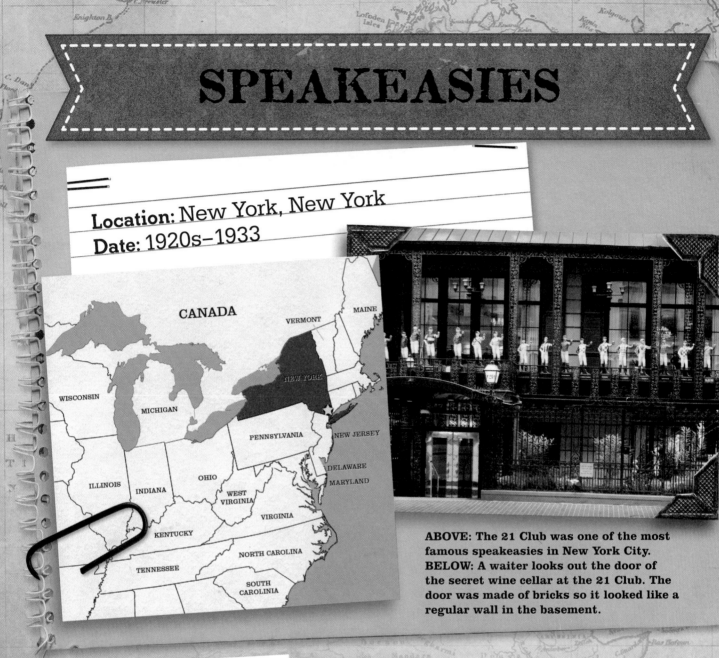

CANADA
MAINE
VERMONT
WISCONSIN
MICHIGAN
NEW YORK
PENNSYLVANIA
NEW JERSEY
ILLINOIS
INDIANA
OHIO
WEST VIRGINIA
DELAWARE
MARYLAND
VIRGINIA
KENTUCKY
NORTH CAROLINA
TENNESSEE
SOUTH CAROLINA

ABOVE: The 21 Club was one of the most famous speakeasies in New York City. BELOW: A waiter looks out the door of the secret wine cellar at the 21 Club. The door was made of bricks so it looked like a regular wall in the basement.

21 CLUB

During an era in American history called Prohibition, alcoholic drinks were illegal. It was a crime to sell or buy alcohol, but that didn't stop some people. Instead, they got beer, wine, and liquor from secret drinking hideouts called speakeasies. One of the most famous speakeasies was the 21 Club. It was a fancy restaurant that also secretly served alcohol. The wine and liquor bottles were kept on special tilting shelves. If the police showed up, the doorman would ring a buzzer to let everyone know there was a raid. The bartenders would then tip the shelves, and the bottles would slide down into secret bins. The club also had a secret wine cellar. It was hidden behind a two-ton door made of bricks. The 21 Club is still open in New York City. The renowned restaurant now sells all kinds of legal beverages, but the secret door is still in the basement.

WHAT'S THE PASSWORD?

The entrance to one of the illegal bars was sometimes a plain door in an alley, where drinkers had to give a secret password or phrase to get in. The password was usually something simple, like "Swordfish" or "Joe sent me." Other speakeasies were disguised as businesses. One New York City speakeasy, called the Park Grill, had a fake bar that sold nonalcoholic drinks. The real bar was upstairs, with a dumbwaiter to bring liquor down to the regular customers. Another New York speakeasy, called the Dixie, was hidden behind a storefront that looked like a cigar shop.

ABOVE: Entrances to speakeasies were often plain, unmarked doors. RIGHT: During Prohibition, an illegal bar was sometimes called a "blind pig."

The word *speakeasy* may have come from "speak-softly shop," an old term for a smuggler's hideout.

Location: Chicago, Illinois
Date: 1928–1931

A GANGSTER'S LAIR

When the United States outlawed alcohol in 1920, a lot of criminals saw a chance to make money. The most notorious of them was Al "Scarface" Capone. From 1928 to 1932, Al Capone ran his criminal empire from the Lexington Hotel on Chicago's South Side. According to Capone legend, the Lexington had many hidden stairways and secret passages. The mob boss used them to go in and out of the hotel without being seen. The entrance to one secret passage was thought to be behind a full-length mirror in Capone's bathroom. Other secret tunnels were rumored to lead under the street to nearby businesses. The Lexington Hotel was demolished in 1996. Workers didn't find any secret passages, but a lot of time had passed and changes had happened since the famous gangster used it as his lair.

ABOVE: In 1986, some people exploring the run-down hotel found a concrete wall in the basement. Who knew what kind of loot might be inside? During a two-hour TV special, they opened the space, but they found only a couple of empty bottles. BELOW: Alphonse Gabriel "Al" Capone was ultimately arrested for tax evasion.

THE MOB BOSS

Al Capone was responsible for some serious crimes, including murder. But he always made sure no evidence connected him to a crime. He also bribed or threatened many officials. The FBI was after him for a long time, but the agents couldn't get any charges to stick. Eventually, the FBI arrested him on a charge he couldn't get out of—not paying taxes on his ill-gotten money. Al Capone was arrested in 1931 and went to prison.

Capone served some of his time at Alcatraz prison.

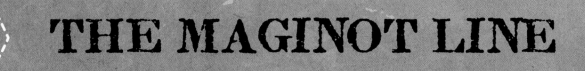
THE MAGINOT LINE

Location: Eastern borders of France

Date: 1928–1945

ABOVE: Sometimes a hideout needs to be secret, but not *too* secret. France wanted its enemies to know the Maginot Line existed, but needed the details and locations of the forts to stay secret. BELOW: The forts were spaced about 9 mi. (14.5 km) apart.

THE UNDERGROUND FORTRESS

In 1919, World War I ended, but the French were worried about what would happen if there was another war. André Maginot convinced the government to build a long line of underground forts, tunnels, and other defenses to protect the country—it was called the Maginot (ma-zhee-NO) Line. The line included more than 100 underground forts. Each fort had its own water supply and backup generators for electricity. There was enough food, water, and fuel for soldiers to stay underground for a month or more with no outside help. Underground bunkers and aboveground defenses, including antitank obstacles and barbed wire fences, were positioned between the forts.

PUTTING IT INTO ACTION

France's fears turned out to be right. Another world war began in 1939, and the Maginot Line's defenses were activated. Some forts had artillery structures at ground level. Those structures had weapons to defend the line from invading armies. The line worked the way it was supposed to, but that didn't stop Germany from invading France. The German army went around the strongest parts of the line. There was also a big gap in the defenses. The builders thought the forest called the Ardennes (ar-DEN) was impossible for an army to get through. They were wrong.

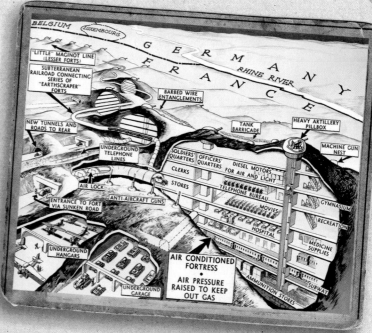

ABOVE: Parts of the fort were more than six stories deep underground. They included offices, barracks, bathrooms, kitchens, and a hospital.
BELOW: The biggest forts had underground railroads for moving people and equipment.

The smaller forts held 100–150 soldiers. The biggest forts held **1,000 or more soldiers.**

ANNE FRANK AND THE SECRET ANNEX

Location: Amsterdam, the Netherlands

Date: 1942–1944

ABOVE: Anne and her family had been living in their hideout for a month and a half when a bookcase was placed in front of the entrance to hide the door.

HIDING FROM THE NAZIS

The Frank family was Jewish. They were from Germany, but when Adolf Hitler came to power, they moved to Amsterdam. When German Nazis invaded the Netherlands, the Frank family moved into a hidden annex in the building where Anne's father, Otto, worked. Anne lived there with her parents and older sister. They shared the hideout with another family of three and an eighth hider. A few non-Jewish helpers from Otto's company brought food, friendship, and news of the outside world. With eight people hiding, they were in constant danger of being discovered. Then, in August 1944, someone betrayed them. The German police arrested everyone in the hideout, along with those who had helped them. The Jews were sent to concentration camps. Only Otto Frank survived.

ABOVE: The secret annex was fairly large as hideouts go. It had five rooms on two floors, along with an attic loft.

Anne and her family lived in their secret hideout for just over **2 years.**

ANNE'S DIARY

On August 21, 1942, 13-year-old Anne Frank wrote in her diary:

"Our hiding place has now become a true hideout. Mr. Kugler thought it would be better to put a bookcase in front of the entrance . . . but of course it's a bookcase that swings on hinges and opens like a door. Mr. Voskuijl did the carpentry."

The world knows about Anne Frank and her family because she kept a diary. In its pages she wrote letters in a diary as if it were a friend named Kitty. She hoped that one day her diary would be published, to tell people of her experiences during the war. When the diary was returned to her father after the war, he honored her memory by making that happen.

THE TEN BOOM HOUSE

Location: Haarlem, the Netherlands
Date: 1943–1944

ABOVE: The hideout was behind a sturdy brick wall that would not sound hollow if it was knocked on.

THE HIDING PLACE

The ten Boom family in Haarlem, the Netherlands, were members of the Dutch underground—a group who helped Jews escape from the Nazi occupiers during World War II. Built into their house was a secret hideout. Concealed behind a false brick wall at the back of Corrie ten Boom's bedroom was a space 3 ft. (1 m) deep. Disguised with old paint, smudges, and a bookcase, it looked as if it had always been part of the house. There was room inside for people to sit or stand, as well as a single mattress to lie on. The hideout was placed in Corrie's room because it was on the third floor of the house. That gave people time to reach the hiding place if the police started their search on the lower floors.

Corrie helped save more than 800 people!

RIGHT: Corrie shows the entrance to the hiding place in her bedroom.

CORRIE TEN BOOM

In the winter of 1944, Corrie ten Boom woke up in the middle of the night to the sound of footsteps running past her bed. She helped six people into the space behind the brick wall and slid the cover panel back into place. She went back to her bed before the German police burst into her room demanding she tell them where the Jews were hiding. Corrie pretended not to know what they were talking about. The secret police arrested Corrie and her father. They never found the six people hiding in her bedroom. Corrie ten Boom was 52 years old at the time of her arrest. She spent the rest of the war in prison camps, but she survived. She received many honors for her resistance work during the war. She lived to the age of 91.

CHEYENNE MOUNTAIN

Location: Colorado Springs, Colorado
Date: 1964–present day

ABOVE: Cheyenne Mountain rises to an elevation of 9,565 ft. (2,915 m). BELOW: The Cheyenne Mountain Complex was built in the 1960s to house a military organization run by the United States and Canada.

THE MOUNTAIN COMPLEX

Like most mountains, Cheyenne Mountain has hiking trails, houses, and resorts. But deep inside this mountain there is a secret hideout. The Cheyenne Mountain Complex is a center for the U.S. Air Force Space Command and houses NORAD, the North American Aerospace Defense Command. The base is deep under the mountain. There are 15 buildings, most of which are three stories tall. It has its own water supply, electric generators, and even a barber shop, medical center, and store. Since the time the base was built, the military and technology needs have changed. In 2008, the main NORAD command center moved to Peterson Air Force Base. Today, the underground base is used as a NORAD training center. But it can instantly take over as the main command for the United States if needed.

The doors are made of steel $3\frac{1}{2}$ feet thick and each weighs **25 tons.**

CLEARANCE 10FT 5IN

ABOVE: The buildings sit on top of more than 1,000 huge, shock-absorbing springs. Two massive blast doors seal the hideout from the outside world. The mountain complex was built to survive a nuclear explosion or massive earthquake. RIGHT: The entrance to the Cheyenne Mountain Complex has been featured in the TV show *Stargate SG-1.*

TRACKING SANTA

In December 1955, the *Colorado Springs Gazette* ran an ad with a telephone number for Santa Claus. But there was a misprint, and the newspaper printed the number for the nearby air defense command operations center instead. Children called that number all evening long on Christmas Eve. The colonel in charge of the center answered the calls and let the young callers know where Santa had last been spotted by radar. The tradition has continued ever since. NORAD tracks Santa's journey every year by radar and satellite.

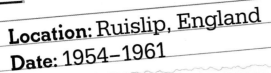

Location: Ruislip, England
Date: 1954–1961

LEFT: The Krogers lived in this house for seven years and became good friends with their neighbors, including the Search family across the street. BELOW: Under the refrigerator was a hidden trap door just big enough for one person. It led to a small cellar where there was a radio transmitter.

THE PORTLAND SPY RING

In 1954, a Canadian couple named Helen and Peter Kroger moved into a small house in Ruislip. They had a shop where they sold rare books in London. But in 1961, the neighborhood got a big surprise—the Krogers were arrested for spying! Their real names were Lona and Morris Cohen. They were spies for the Soviet Union. Several hidden compartments full of equipment were found in their house. The Krogers were part of a five-member group known as the Portland Spy Ring. Their job was to receive stolen information gathered from the Isle of Portland, where weapons were developed for the British submarine fleet. They relayed that information via the radio in their cellar to agents in Moscow. What the Krogers didn't know was that the British Security Service had been watching them for months from their neighbor's house. All five members of the spy ring were arrested.

THE KROGERS . . . OR REALLY THE COHENS

Being part of the Portland Spy Ring wasn't the Krogers' first job for the KGB. In the 1940s, as Lona and Morris Cohen, they passed information to the Soviet Union about the United States' nuclear weapons program. When a pair of their fellow spies were arrested, the Cohens escaped to Mexico. They eventually ended up in Moscow, where they were trained for their new mission in England. After their arrest in England, the Krogers were sentenced to 20 years in prison. After eight years, the British government sent them to the Soviet Union as part of a prisoner exchange. The Krogers, or the Cohens, lived the rest of their lives in Moscow.

In their London bookstore, the Krogers were passed film, documents, and other items by KGB spies.

ABOVE: Secret compartments were found throughout the Krogers' house. A powerful radio antenna along with cameras and other photo equipment were stashed in the attic. The house's bathroom doubled as a darkroom for developing film. BELOW: The Krogers departing for Moscow.

PIRATE RADIO

Location: Southwest coast of England
Date: 1964–1967

RIGHT: Broadcasting at sea wasn't always fun. Sometimes the DJs got seasick. BELOW: There were no CDs, MP3s, or computers then, so most of the music came from vinyl records like these playing on turntables. The bouncing of the ship sometimes made the needle skip.

RADIO CAROLINE

On Easter Sunday 1964, radio listeners in southern England heard a new station. "This is Radio Caroline on 199," the announcer said, "your all-day music station." By British law the broadcast was illegal. In the 1960s, the British Broadcasting Corporation (BBC) was the only broadcaster allowed on the air in Britain. It played plenty of news and entertainment programs, but only six hours of pop music a week. There was no real way for new bands to get their music on the radio. So a group of DJs and radio engineers set up stations where the government couldn't touch them: on ships anchored in the ocean. The broadcasts started with two ships and stations: Radio Caroline from the ship MV *Caroline* and Radio Atlanta from the MV *Mi Amigo*. Their broadcasts reached almost half the people in England. But because the ships were anchored in international waters, the British government had no power to stop them.

LEFT: Radio Caroline DJs (left to right): Paul Noble, Jon Sydney, Keith Skues, Colin Nicol, and Bryan Vaughan.

THE RADIO CAROLINE LEGACY

Eventually, radio ships from other countries sailed to England to anchor offshore and broadcast their programs. Fed up with the radio pirates, the British government passed a new law in 1967. The law made it a crime for anyone in Britain to give music, programming, advertising, food, water, or fuel to the operators of offshore radio stations. With no one in the country allowed to help them, most of the ship-based stations closed down. However, Radio Caroline is still on the air. Its programming can be heard all over the world, streaming on the Internet.

The first song played on Radio Caroline was the Rolling Stones song "Not Fade Away."

RIGHT: Radio Caroline ship today.

Location: Berlin, Germany
Date: 1964

ABOVE: Guards along the Berlin wall would arrest or possibly shoot those trying to escape. BELOW: The east side of the wall belonged to communist East Germany. The west side belonged to democratic West Germany. The wall kept the two separate.

THE CROSSING

Horst Breistoffer waited to cross the border between communist East Berlin and democratic West Berlin. The city was divided in half by a tall concrete wall, which kept the people of East Berlin from leaving. Border guards examined cars and trucks carefully to make sure people were not hiding inside. Horst thought they would pay less attention to a small car. He sat nervously behind the wheel of a strange-looking minicar called an Isetta wondering if his clever plan would work. Horst had modified his little car so a passenger could hide in the back! As Horst pulled up to the barrier, he handed the guard his passport. The guard checked his papers, gave the bubble car a short once-over, and waved him through. Horst and his secret cargo had made it!

THE LAST TRIP

Horst Breistoffer made nine successful people-smuggling trips across the border using two different Isettas. On his tenth trip, the woman hiding in the back moved while the car was at the checkpoint. The Isetta rocked on its wheels, and the jig was up. Both Horst and his passenger were arrested.

ABOVE: Horst removed the air intake, battery, and heater. He moved the exhaust pipe, and put in a plywood platform to create just enough space to hide a passenger.

The car's bulbous shape and curved windows earned it the nickname "bubble car."

LEFT: The door on the Isetta was the whole front of the car. It also had a motor the size of a basketball.

UNDERGROUND CINEMA

Location: Paris, France
Date: Middle Ages–present day

ABOVE: After passing a Do Not Enter sign, the policemen who found the underground movie theater heard dogs barking. The sound turned out to be a recording, intended to frighten people away.

THE CATACOMBS

In 2004, a group of policemen went through a drain tunnel into the catacombs under Paris on a training mission. They stumbled upon a cave with seats built into the rock, a movie screen, projector, and sound system. It was a complete movie theater, 60 ft. (18 m) underground! Nearby was another cave with tables, chairs, a bar, and a cooker. The whole area was wired for electricity and telephones. The police left, confused. But when they returned three days later, everything was gone. The only thing left in the empty cave was a note. It read: *Don't look for us.*

The tunnels under Paris were created when miners carved out stones to build the city. They are often called catacombs, but only some of the underground spaces house the bones of the dead.

ABOVE: In the late 1700s and early 1800s, when cemeteries throughout Paris got too full, the bones were dug up and brought into the tunnels.

EXTREME ART

A small part of the catacombs is open for visitors, but the rest of the underground network is off-limits. Anyone caught there is fined. But people still sneak into the underground world. Some have secret parties, make art, or paint the walls with graffiti. It turned out that the secret movie theater hideout was a project created by a group called the UX, which stands for Urban eXperiment. It's a group of artists who explore, work, and put on secret shows in the tunnels under the city. They also do restoration work in the caves and tunnels. But because they're going where they're not supposed to, they get in trouble if they're caught.

There are more than
**150 mi.
(241.5 km)**
of tunnels, caves, and passageways under the streets and buildings of Paris.

LEFT: Some people paint or graffiti the tunnel walls. BELOW: People who explore or sneak around the catacombs are called "cataphiles," or catacomb lovers.

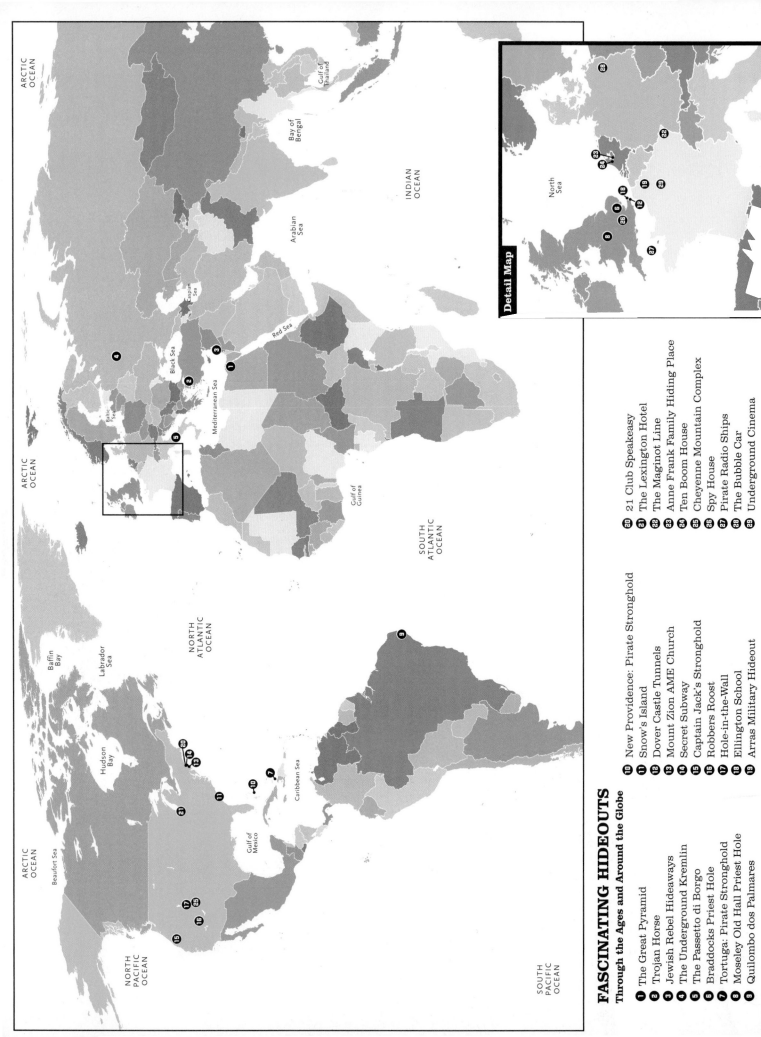

FASCINATING HIDEOUTS
Through the Ages and Around the Globe

1 The Great Pyramid
2 Trojan Horse
3 Jewish Rebel Hideaways
4 The Underground Kremlin
5 The Passetto di Borgo
6 Braddocks Priest Hole
7 Tortuga: Pirate Stronghold
8 Moseley Old Hall Priest Hole
9 Quilombo dos Palmares

10 New Providence: Pirate Stronghold
11 Snow's Island
12 Dover Castle Tunnels
13 Mount Zion AME Church
14 Secret Subway
15 Captain Jack's Stronghold
16 Robbers Roost
17 Hole-in-the-Wall
18 Ellington School
19 Arras Military Hideout

20 21 Club Speakeasy
21 The Lexington Hotel
22 The Maginot Line
23 Anne Frank Family Hiding Place
24 Ten Boom House
25 Cheyenne Mountain Complex
26 Spy House
27 Pirate Radio Ships
28 The Bubble Car
29 Underground Cinema

Detail Map